Commodity Women

Commodity Women

A Daring Journey into the Mind-
Set of *Some* Women

Anastasio Nasa, M.Sc.

iUniverse LLC
Bloomington

COMMODITY WOMEN
A Daring Journey into the Mind-Set of *Some* Women

http://www.commoditywomen.com
commoditywomen@yahoo.com
First edition published in March 2011

iUniverse books may be ordered through booksellers or by contacting:

iUniverse
1663 Liberty Drive
Bloomington, IN 47403
www.iuniverse.com
1-800-Authors (1-800-288-4677)

Because of the dynamic nature of the Internet, any web addresses or links contained in this book may have changed since publication and may no longer be valid. The views expressed in this work are solely those of the author and do not necessarily reflect the views of the publisher, and the publisher hereby disclaims any responsibility for them.

Any people depicted in stock imagery provided by Thinkstock are models, and such images are being used for illustrative purposes only.

Certain stock imagery © Thinkstock.

ISBN: 978-1-4917-0838-5 (sc)
ISBN: 978-1-4917-0840-8 (hc)
ISBN: 978-1-4917-0839-2 (e)

Library of Congress Control Number: 2013916855

Printed in the United States of America.

iUniverse rev. date: 10/11/2013

Dedication

To all the women in the world who maintain an inner beauty that will last beyond age and time. This beauty provides a power that will remain when everything else vanishes. I dedicate this book to you, even though it does not address you. Your spiritual and feminine ways make me open doors for you and carry your luggage. Your demure nature melts my heart and causes me to do whatever you ask. Your understanding of my vulnerable ego inspires me to place you on a pedestal, above criticism, and beyond any doubts. Your spiritual support will last after material power fades away, when friends depart, health declines, and money dwindles. Your tenderness gives me strength, your patience fills me with courage, and your understanding instills in me the confidence to mature and grow. Your spirit will always be with me, in this life and beyond.

Table of Contents

Preface

This book is geared toward men in their twenties. The information I offer is relevant to their daily lives and especially valuable now while they are in their mid-twenties and puzzled by *some* women's behavior. If the young prefer to learn the hard way, they will acquire this knowledge by their mid-fifties; however, it will be too late to use it. The knowledge in this book took me a long time to gather and process, requiring almost a lifetime of experience, research, and travel. I wish I had the opportunity to use this knowledge when I most needed it. When I look back at myself in my twenties, I see innocence, ignorance, immaturity, high expectations, miscommunication, and misunderstanding. Thus I decided to share what I have learned with young people, who most need it. Unfortunately, a lot of people who have learned the hard way choose not to share what they know with the young. That's because they are in direct competition with them. Young people have the asset of youth, while older people have the advantage of experience. The combination of youth and experience should provide the reader with a competitive edge that each group on its own does not enjoy.

Introduction

Have you ever wondered why some women behave in unpredictable ways, as if there are no rules governing their behavior? Have you been puzzled by a sudden, seemingly illogical change in your woman's mood? If so, then this book is for you. This latest attempt at solving an eternal puzzle is backed by twenty years of research, investigation, and in-depth analysis. I believe I have finally cracked the eternal puzzle.

What Is the Puzzle?

Why do women do what they do? What are their motives? What do they really want? Why does a woman who says she wants a nice guy chooses the exact opposite? Why do nice guys finish last? Why do I seem to attract more women when I already have one? What makes a woman lead on several guys when she is not interested in any of them? Why is she friendlier with strangers while in the company of her man? Why is it that she does not know what she wants; only what she doesn't want? Why is it that hell has no fury like a woman scorned? Why does she complain about being viewed as a sex object while behaving and dressing like one? What does she like about this guy? Why is she attracted to power symbols—fancy cars, fame, and wealth? Does she have a sixth sense? How does she use it? How can you detect it and defeat it? How do we know what a woman really wants if what she wants and what she gets attached to are two different things? The answers to all of these questions and more are presented in chapter 4.

The Rosetta Stone

I solved the puzzle by using a fresh set of eyes and senses and by thinking outside of the box of reason, logic, and common sense. I took a new analytical approach, comparing the behavior of *some* women with similar patterns of behavior attributed to a familiar system. Comparing the two patterns allowed me to fill in the gaps of the puzzle, understand the roots of certain actions, and predict the behavior of these women. The process was similar to solving the unknown hieroglyphic language by comparing its content with the other known languages having the same content carved on the Rosetta stone, discovered a little over two centuries ago.

The comparable language or metaphor used in this study is quite familiar but had not yet been fully utilized to explore women's behavior. Through a stroke of luck, I started to pay attention to this metaphor and explore its dimensions. A woman I was dating told me emphatically that she was very "expensive." Her expression led me to examine the mentality of a commodity item. What if commodities could feel, think, plan, and manipulate the market? Wouldn't they claim higher market values? Wouldn't they attempt to suppress competitors or even eliminate them? Wouldn't they try to control and reshape consumers' minds to their own advantage? What an interesting subject to investigate— the minds of *some* women! I will explore issues concerning commodity-minded women alone. The term *some women* could cover a range from 1 percent to 99 percent, and I will leave it up to the reader to determine the percentage that best represents his own experience. In short, I intend to provide an in-depth analysis of why some women do what they do and to shed light on communication problems that have puzzled humanity since the dawn of civilization. More research is needed to learn how to use this knowledge to expedite the evolutionary process and liberate some women from the commodity mind that is deeply engraved in their psyches.

Chapter 1:

The Metaphor

Give a man a fish and you feed him for a day; teach a man to fish and you feed him for a lifetime.

—Chinese proverb

The task of analyzing the commodity mind seemed overwhelming at first, but as I learned more about commodity markets, it became easier to figure out the answers. I studied marketing strategies and rules in an attempt to find parallels that would crack the puzzle. The more I learned about negotiations, marketing, advertising, packaging, consumer behavior, and sales tactics the more I became convinced that I had selected the correct means of explanation: the commodity-market metaphor.

Commodities are articles of trade that are subject to market rules that have evolved throughout history and become part of daily life in the market. Commodity-market rules have been limited to material objects and have rarely been applied to human behavior. Until now, no attempt has been made to explore what a commodity would do if "she" could think and act and had the sophistication, intelligence, education, knowledge, experience, resources, power, and desire to manipulate the market to "her" advantage.

Forgive my use of the words *she* and *her* in reference to a commodity! However, this study is based on the assumption that *some* women behave as a commodity would if animated and given the chance to act on free will. I will refer to these women as commodity-minded women. The women to whom I dedicated this book do not think and behave like commodities and are not covered since they present no puzzle. They communicate in a straightforward, unambiguous way to which others can easily relate.

This study suggests that the puzzling behavior of commodity-minded women most often stems from insecurity about their market value, which they attempt to protect. For example, when a woman senses the danger of getting dumped, she will act first and become the dumper rather than wait and risk becoming the one dumped. When she takes the initiative to end a relationship, her behavior puzzles the man she has just dumped. He might think that he did nothing to deserve her rejection. In reality, he took actions that threatened her stability, though he did not recognize this. Her sharp sixth sense coupled with her insecurity left her feeling cornered, prompting her to make a preemptive strike against the potential threat.

To make things more puzzling, she will never tell him the reasons behind her abrupt decision. She will never tell him that she sensed a threat and acted first because she feared that her market value might be undermined. If she admitted that, it would defeat the purpose of preserving her market value in the first place and would show her insecurity and vulnerability. Instead, she will offer another explanation that justifies her action while preserving her market value. "My ex-boyfriend is back in town," she might say, or "I just met this wonderful man who pushed the right buttons and generated instantaneous chemistry and attraction." You will never hear her say, "When you did not call me for two days, I thought that you didn't want me anymore and I had to dump you first to protect my market value and my image." Her behavior will be seen as puzzling because it does not match the common-sense pattern of people without insecurities about their market value. A man must understand his woman's sensitivity and adjust his behavior to account for her insecurity and give her continual assurance of her market worth. In doing so, a man can enjoy the fruits of a woman's sense of security instead of spending his life time complaining, wondering, and attempting to understand her puzzling behavior.

While many publications focus on relationship recipes, offering readers dos and don'ts, this study goes deeper into the commodity mind of *some* women, explaining the roots of their behavior. If you understand the roots of a problem, you can customize a solution to suit your circumstances. I choose to offer you fishing skills rather than feed you a fish. Once you understand the root cause of women's behavior, you will be able to intelligently create your own cure and get better results.

With the commodity-market metaphor established as a pivotal point in this study, I want to explore how this metaphor can be utilized to understand commodity-minded women's behavior. Business rules can be safely applied to solve the puzzle. The areas of sales, marketing, and negotiations offer parallels with cause-and-effect relationships and can provide answers. However, I do not suggest in any way that women should be treated like commodities or thought of as such. This study simply explains why despite the liberation of women and their tremendous achievement in gaining freedom and equality, *some* of them retain a commodity mind-set that evolved under strict social conditions and has lasted for tens of thousands of years. To survive such conditions, women had to evolve in a certain direction and develop a mentality that sustained their influence and ensured their survival. That is the commodity mind.

While enjoying the fruits of their recent liberation, some women still hold on dearly to the old commodity mind-set and therefore come across as having dual personalities, that of a human being and that of a commodity. Alternating between those two personalities seems to give them more flexibility while adding a smoke screen to the already puzzling behavior of a commodity-minded woman. The challenge of converting from a commodity mind to a human mind is similar to the challenge facing a student learning a new language but behaving in his own native language's culture.

While learning to speak the new language, he is still thinking, feeling, and expressing himself based on his native culture and social training. He might be able to put words together and form a grammatically correct sentence in the new language. However, he won't be able to form a sentence reflecting the new culture unless he is liberated from his native language and exposed long enough to the social training that goes hand in hand with the language he is learning.

Some men experience self-doubt after failing in a relationship. Those who were too lenient with their women tend to think that they should have been bossier to sustain the relationship. Others who might have been strict and cold toward their women think that they should have been softer and more lenient. While self-doubt is a normal reaction to the collapse of a relationship, dwelling on your inadequacies could become self-destructive and could lead to a misunderstanding of the root cause of failure. Swinging back and forth between a sweet nature and a tough personality is not the answer. You need to examine a failed relationship in light of the commodity mind metaphor. In most cases, the real reason behind relationship failure has something to do with compromising the market value of the woman. The relationship could have failed simply because the woman found a prospect who would better enhance her market value and make her look hotter. A relationship doesn't fail because you have been too nice or too big a jerk, even if your self-doubt or her accusations make it seem so. Of course she will never tell you the real reasons or say, "Oh, I am sorry. I just met another man who makes me look hotter than you do. I would like to hook him for a long-term commitment until I find a hotter man. Bye."

Actually, if you are serious about maintaining or improving a relationship, you must boost or at least maintain the market value of your woman. You also have to watch for any developing relationships that might become serious enough to grant her the desired rise in her market value. Some commodity-minded women find it more lucrative to get a divorce than to stay married. Others decide it is better to stay wed. However, they will eventually pursue the option leading to their optimum market value. No wonder divorce rates are astronomical.

Chapter 2:

Blame It on Evolution

If you want to test a man's character, give him power.

—*Abraham Lincoln*

The single most important asset for a commodity-minded woman to nurture and protect is her market value. The more you promote her value (actively, not verbally) the more she will love you. Her goal is to catch the guy with the highest possible value she can get. If you succeed in making her feel that her market value is promoted in your company, then she is all yours. A commodity-minded woman will love you to the extent that you can raise her market value among her peers and competitors. That does not mean that you have to spend a whole lot of money on her (unless it is the only way for her to display a high market value). Her market value could be enhanced by getting attached to a celebrity, a popular person, an executive in a high position, the class teacher, a politician, the president of the United States, or an ordinary man married to a beautiful woman, etc.

She could achieve the same goal by getting acquainted with a race or a class known to be fashionable or having high stature. A new breed of women known as cougars gets a kick out of dating younger men and enjoying the admiration and jealousy of other women. Cougars seem to be saying, "I am still hot and desirable enough that I can attract and keep this young kid as a lover." These women are most likely high-maintenance commodities looking and acting much younger than they are, thanks to extreme makeover technology and wrinkle-removal cosmetics and other secret strategies. If she is forty but looks twenty-five, she will make the demands of a woman with a twenty-five-year-old's market value. One of those demands is to be dating a twenty-five- to thirty-year-old dude who has a market value comparable to the one she claims.

If a man has nothing to offer other than money, the commodity-minded woman he is dating will demand more of it in pursuit of her enhanced image and then brag about getting it. She will tell her girlfriends how much money he has spent on her and name the fancy restaurants where they have dined. Once, while in the gym working out, I overheard two girls in their twenties exchanging stories emphasizing their market values. One girl told the other that she was wined and dined in well-known restaurants by several guys and hadn't spent a penny from her own pocket. She never mentioned how appreciative she was that they had done this. She was clearly elevating her market value to impress her competitor girlfriend, who responded with a more compelling story in the same vein.

Some might argue that this behavior is driven by a materialistic culture and would not occur in more spiritual cultures. But to paraphrase Abraham Lincoln, "if you want to test a woman's character, give her power". There is no doubt that contemporary Western women have the most power ever possessed by women and therefore could well reveal the real character of their gender. Women living under the tyranny of other cultures' customs and taboos would refrain from boasting the way the two girls in the gym did. However, women of other cultures may attempt to enhance their market value in subtler ways, providing no help in solving the puzzle. For example, Japanese women smile when they are angry and when they are happy. How can you know their true feeling? In more traditional societies women will veil and display innocence to meet their market standards.

It is no coincidence that women with high market value end up associating with wealthy and powerful men. After all, behind every great man is a woman who is probably helping him move up, eventually raising her own market value as well.

How did these women end up like this? Who made them this way? Is such behavior hard-wired in their DNA or the result of social training? Or is it a combination of both?

Since men are the end users of commodity-minded women, men must have invented the concept of market value and imposed it on these poor women, expecting them to live up to this twisted standard. For example, in the ancient traditional society of the desert the dowry given to the father of a bride included camels or other property. The value of the dowry would most likely correspond to the value of the bride, an economic factor that probably contributed to the extreme emphasis on women's virginity in traditional societies. Since market criteria vary from one society to another, this analysis will focus on Western women, who represent the real character of women when acting of their own free will.

Years ago when I was in my twenties, I attended a party

and wound up spending most of my time in conversation with an interesting American lady. She was a bit overweight, but this did not detract from her winning personality, inner beauty, and intriguing intellect. With the party winding down and only a few guests remaining in the house, the host jokingly asked me about the woman, sarcastically referring to her as "your girlfriend." I smiled, confirming to him that she was a very nice person. Still, his counter response opened my eyes to the concept of market value and the existence of market standards. Yes, I was naive back then.

He told me, "She has to be nice. She is fat." Did that mean she was faking amiability to compensate for the low market value caused by her physical appearance? If so, I couldn't blame her. She was a victim of the market criteria established by men such as Glenn, my host. I could not respond to him at the time. If I see him today, I would tell him that if a woman's market value is a function of her physical appearance, then a man's market value corresponds to his wallet and that he has an empty one. I certainly did not like what he said. But it is what it is. Ultimately, some women have fallen into the trap set by men and have ended up thinking and acting like commodities. It's worth looking at this sad fact to learn how a commodity woman behaves to enhance her market value and increase her chances of attracting the highest bidder.

Once you realize that you are dealing with such women, you can master the art of relating to them if you apply commodity-market standards concerning sales, marketing, pricing, negotiations, competition, packaging, advertising, supply and demand, inflation, recession, discounts, depreciation, salvage value, and even taxes and net worth. No wonder car salesmen have a high rate of success with these women!

I believe there is a genetic explanation for the evolution of the market rules initiated by men, the prime consumer of this commodity. Long ago through the course of evolution, the genetic pool probably offered an equal chance to men who liked young women and to men who liked older women. The genes of those who liked young women survived and spread more quickly because young women are more fertile than older women. As a result, most contemporary men prefer dating younger women, and they impose the law of supply and demand on those women's minds. In addition, promiscuous men of ancient times spread their genes faster than monogamous men did. While a monogamous man could pass down his genes once every nine months (or twice if he fathered twins), a promiscuous man might pass his genes down the line more than twice a week. That is almost eighty times faster. In a life span of a monogamous man he can impregnate his woman no more than twenty times. Otherwise she will have serious health problems.

Assuming a twenty-year separation between generations, it is possible to calculate the rates at which the genes of monogamous and promiscuous men are spread. In year one, a monogamous man produces one child (with nine months of pregnancy and three months of recovery between pregnancies). In year twenty, he produces his twentieth child. By year sixty, his twentieth child (now forty years old) produces the four-hundredth grandchild. By year one hundred, his four-hundredth grandchild produces his eight-thousandth great-grandchild. So a motivated monogamous man and his motivated descendants can yield eight thousand descendants in a hundred years of uninterrupted production. 1x20x20x20 = 8000 children.

Similar assumptions for the promiscuous man (with a production rate eighty times greater than a monogamous man's) will yield the following calculation. 1x(80x20) x(80x20)x(80x20) = 4,096,000,000 children. That is 4,096,000,000 / 8000 = 512,000 times as many as the monogamous man produces in one hundred years. So in a hundred years, there will be 512,000 promiscuous children for every monogamous child in a given population's genetic pool. The two per million monogamy rate would exponentially diminish over a few centuries, and the trait would disappear from the gene pool within four hundred years. With the world population approaching seven billion, the monogamous gene must have gone extinct a long time ago. Therefore, monogamous men who, if existed would be considered ultra-civil in their practice of self-control and should be treated as an endangered species.

Though these astronomical figures do not practically happen in the real world, the theory holds true for any reproduction rates both kinds of men in fact adopted. At any reproduction rate, monogamy genes would eventually go extinct, leaving 100 percent of contemporary men carrying the promiscuity gene down the line. Although the promiscuity gene is alive and kicking in all contemporary men, social training, limited resources, and the rise of religion and ethics in contemporary societies have suppressed promiscuity to a great extent. These factors have compelled contemporary men to behave themselves and look after the welfare of their offspring by practicing self-control to the best of their abilities.

Furthermore, today's gene pool was cumulated over millions of years through uninterrupted lines running through generations of ancestors all the way back to algae, not just humans. Millions of years are enough time to increase the concentration of the promiscuity gene incrementally and wipe out any trace of the monogamy gene from the gene pool.

As for ancient women, whether monogamous or promiscuous, both types had an equal opportunity to pass their genes once a year (nine months of pregnancy and three months for recovery). Therefore, we find both types of women in the gene pool today, with a fifty-fifty market share.

So 100 percent of men and 50 percent of women are coded to be promiscuous. Adding insult to injury, male-dominated cultures throughout history have curtailed the freedom of women in sexual relationships while giving men license to enter multiple marriages and promiscuous relationships. Under these challenging conditions, women have had no choice but to compete with each other to survive men's appetite and control of the market, therefore developing the commodity mind and commodity-market standards.

During the ordeal of Bill Clinton and Monica Lewinsky, I defended Clinton with this argument. *Most men inherited the promiscuity gene while most women did not. That is because ancient promiscuous men succeeded in passing their genes to us three times a week, not once every nine months. That being the case, when a man has an affair with a second lady, he does not necessarily intend to cheat on the first lady. When a woman does the same thing, she most likely intends to hurt her man. Some cultures allowed multiple marriages to solve this problem. Let's judge Clinton by nature's standards, because he is a man.* **Let's blame it on evolution.**

Chapter 3:

A Dozen Rules

Life's a game. All you have to do is know how to play it.

—Unknown

In this chapter, I will offer a dozen rules to review on your way to meeting your date.

1. **A commodity-minded woman will do anything at any time for no logical reason.**

Be prepared so you won't be taken by surprise. She might not show up. She could go to the bathroom and never return. She could come back but get an urgent phone call saying that her roommate burned down the house twice and have to leave. She could meet a stranger on her way back and leave with him instead of you. She could suddenly jump out of her seat and decide to leave while still chewing on her food. She could ask you to give her a ride to the middle of nowhere to sit and pray to the stars. She could turn into a pumpkin even before midnight! Use your imagination and expect her to do the most bizarre thing. Then you won't be disappointed.

2. **The more leverage (power) you give her the more she'll use it against you.**

Power corrupts, and absolute power corrupts absolutely. This maxim also applies to power leverage in relationships.

3. **Commodity-minded women don't know what they want. They only know what they don't want.**

I heard this from a woman with Ph.D. in international politics. I heard it over and over from other women when they were confronted with a puzzling question: what do you want? Mel Gibson's movie *What Women Want* was a comedy but revealed many truths about some women's thoughts. I recommend seeing it.

4. **A woman will abandon her man as soon as she feels his dependence on her.**

Let your actions say, "I am interested, but I can do without you." I once asked a woman what was wrong with being a nice guy, and she said, "Being nice by itself is not bad. It is the sense that the man needs the woman more than she needs him that qualifies him for rejection." A woman will tell you that she wants a man who needs her, then dump you as soon as you show her exactly that. Let your woman feel that you like her but can also do without her, and she will never leave you alone.

5. **What women want in a man is different from what they get attached to.**

This is the factor that makes commodity women's behavior so puzzling. A man's inability to distinguish between what women like and what they get attached to makes them a mystery. Of course a woman likes it when you tell her sweet things, shower her with gifts, and say how beautiful she is. Of course she likes it when you clean up her mess, pay her bills, and spend your money on her. She likes everything that you do for her, but that doesn't mean that she likes you. She likes what you do but gets attached to something else. The man she will get attached to and fall in love with might not have done any of the things you did for her. He could be a bum who has nothing to offer, but for some reason he makes her feel that he is a winner who sends her market value soaring. She might even end up supporting him for that.

6. A woman's sixth sense is real and very powerful.

Don't ever underestimate the intensity and power of a woman's sixth sense. Be prepared to deal with it. The more you account for its power the more you are equipped to dissipate it and defeat it. You can even control it to your advantage to sense your wrong information and leave her totally off balance. Have you noticed how some women can observe everything happening around them without looking directly at the area under investigation? A woman looks somewhere near you (almost where her blind spot is, if she looks directly at you) in order to track your moves. She seems to have a second pair of eyes near her ears or in the back of her head! Have you also noticed how she relaxes her body, showing you some interesting parts and making you feel at ease to check them out, then suddenly turning her head and catching you in the act of staring?

How embarrassing! Be careful and never underestimate this amazing power. Experienced men treat women's sixth sense with respect and guard themselves against it. You need to acknowledge its power and then gradually learn to adjust to it and use it to your advantage.

7. **"How do you write woman so well? I think of a man and I take away reason and accountability", Jack Nicholson.**

In the movie *As Good as It Gets*, Jack Nicholson is a writer famous for dealing with women's issues. A lady asks him, "How do you write women so well?" and he replies, "I think of a man and I take away reason and accountability." There is a reason for women's behavior that Nicholson's character cannot recognize. It is like infrared waves, which exist but are invisible to the eye. Similarly, there are reasons for women's behavior, but they can't be deciphered by using ordinary common sense. That's because they operate under a different set of rules, the rules of the commodity market. For example, when a woman calls at the last minute to cancel a date or simply does not show up, what is her reason? She might offer a seemingly plausible excuse, but the real reason is most likely that she did not feel glamorous enough to impress you. She might be a bit overweight or tired with dark circles under her eyes, etc. Any of these physical flaws could affect her market value and could be the real reason, but she will never tell you that. She just can't! You've got to figure it out on your own and accept it. If you try to enforce or even encourage accountability, she will label you as a control freak. Experienced men have given up and learned to live with this behavior, and they have plan B or plan C in case of accountability malfunction. Plan for the worst and hope for the best.

8. A commodity-minded woman is like a seat belt: you have to pull it slowly to get it to come your way.

   If you force it, it will freeze on you.

9. The more beautiful the woman is (large breasts, sexy, or high market value), the more these rules apply.

10. A woman wants a man who *genuinely* does not want her.

11. Market value to a woman is as important as ego to a man.

12. A man is after the best match. A woman is after the best catch.

   There are only a few exceptions to these rules. For egotistic reasons, men will sometimes tell me, *"May be you are just judging from your own experience or the kind of women you have met. But my woman is different. She is an exception to these rules."* A few months later, they return, tell me their stories, and say, *"I hate to admit it, but you were right."*

Chapter 4:

FAQ about Women

Adults are always asking kids what they want to be when they grow up, because they're looking for ideas.
— *Paula Poundstone*

Nice Guys or Bad Boys?

1. **Why does a woman say that she wants a nice man who cares about her and treats her with respect but then get attached to a man who does the exact opposite, even abusing her?**

The traditional answer to this question is that women who act like this have low self-esteem and therefore end up in abusive relationships that correspond to this poor self-image. The truth is this: a woman will compromise herself in hopes of catching the biggest fish available. The difficulty of the mission increases with the value of the prey. In fact, abuse may confirm to her that she is about to bait a big fish that is trying to slip away. The abuse she is experiencing could be likened to the slapping struggle of a fish when hooked to the fishing rod. It is a sign of success, not failure. The fish that does not struggle is either dead or not yet hooked, so is the man who does not abuse her. If a woman disliked abusive behavior, she would do something to stop it. A market value issue keeps her in pursuit of her struggling but highly valued prey. While putting up with his abuse, she is thinking, *No pain, no gain.*

Of her own free will, this woman will pursue the man who promotes her market value more than any other man does, regardless of his abusive behavior. After all, women do not have ego problems like men do. Market value is for women what ego is for men. A woman would give away her ego to gain a higher market value.

2. Why do nice guys finish last or get ditched first?

This is one of the most puzzling questions men face. How often have you heard a nice guy say, "Despite everything I did for her, she dumped me"? He will recall how good he was to a woman and how much he loved her, giving her his full attention, showering her with gifts, remaining faithful to her, and catering to her needs, only to find her running off with another man!

It's not despite; it's because

Here is the answer: it is not despite; it is because. Yes, it is not despite providing for her, that she abandoned him. It is because of his intense attention and care that she abandoned him. When you pet a cat too much, she walks away, but when you leave her alone she comes back and sits on your lap. Here is how it works in the mind of a commodity-minded woman. Nice guys get rejected not because they are nice but because they signal despair and dependence, motivating the commodity-minded woman to look for the next bid up. In a real-life auction, once you place a bid, the auctioneer puts you on hold and pursues other offers until he finds the highest bidder. Similarly, a nice guy gives away his value too soon, leading a woman to put him on the back burner while she searches for the highest bidder. If you hang in there on the back burner, she might get back to you if she has found no higher bid than yours. But if you chase her like a puppy, you might be asked to leave the room.

Good news for nice guys

There is nothing wrong with being nice. What is wrong is being desperate. Revealing your intentions too soon will land you on the back burner. And if you haunt a woman desperately, she will feel that you need her more than she needs you and then dump you. The happy medium is to be nice but not desperate. An overanxious man is a turnoff for a woman. His behavior signals that he believes he has found a good deal in dating her. To the commodity mind, a good deal is something worth more than you got it for. It's cheap. No woman wants to be seen as cheap or as a good deal for somebody. How do you think a car would feel if sold below its market value? A woman wants to find a good deal, not provide one. She will dump you the minute you make her feel that you see her as a good deal. I am not suggesting that you make her feel that she is a terrible deal. That would not work either. Maintain a happy medium where you keep nice and gentle but not desperate.

While learning about negotiation techniques, I came across an analogy worth noting. Assume that you are buying a used car from a dealer who quotes an initial price of $10,000. You make an offer of $3,000, and the salesman immediately accepts it. How would you feel, and what would you do? You will probably think there must be something wrong with the car, and you decide not to buy it. Your decision has nothing to do with the condition of the car. It has more to do with the poor presentation by the novice salesman.

Now, let's consider a different scenario for the same car with an experienced salesman, who also quotes a $10,000 price. After you offer $3,000, this salesman gives you an astonished look and raises his eyebrows. He mumbles a few words expressing how ridiculous your offer is. He might even pull away from the sale, claiming he has better things to do. Now you feel more comfortable about the car condition and raise your bid to $5,500. The salesman on his way leaving the office turns his head to you saying few more words showing disappointment but is now rather conciliatory. He counters with a price of $8,000 after consulting his imaginary boss and looking up few charts claiming that he is making a big sacrifice to help you. Now how do you feel? You want to lop off a few more dollars and offer $6,500. The salesman shows a bit of frustration but offers you a final deal of $7,500 without warranty and adds a condition to finish the transaction and take the car out of the lot the same day. You end up buying the car for $7,000 and take it home, telling your friends how clever a buyer you were in reducing the price 30 percent and driving the salesman up the wall.

You are happy not because the car condition is better than it was before, but because the salesman succeeded in installing the sense of victory in you and making you feel that you had gotten a good deal. Your satisfaction has nothing to do with the real value or condition of the car. It is all about how you ran the show in negotiating the deal and installing the sense of winning in your adversary. A car dealer once taught me a lesson about the importance of people skills in the sales profession. He asked me if I knew the difference between rape and romance. After listening to my lengthy response, he finally gave me his answer. "Presentation," he said.

Now let's go back to nice guys dilemma. Nice guys are similar to the novice salesman who reduced the price by 70 percent in one shot and therefore scared away the customer. How do you think a woman will feel when you reduce your value and act out of desperation? Instead of proposing plans for travel, partnering, helping out, dining, and movies in a first encounter with a woman, an experienced man will take one step at a time, monitoring her reaction and giving her the sense that she is winning. There is nothing wrong with doing that. You are not misrepresenting your value to her but protecting it from the sudden depreciation that could result from poor presentation. Instead of showing your hand too soon, showering her with gifts, e-mails, and telephone calls, relax and give her a chance to feel that she is winning in pursuing you. Let me say this one more time, there is nothing wrong about being nice. Just don't act anxious or desperate. Remember that she is out to find the highest bidder, so give her a chance to feel that the highest bidder is you. And even after you establish an intimate relationship; give her room to miss you once in a while. It is important for her to always feel that you are still and will always be the best offer.

A window of opportunity is a window of moderation

One word of caution: do not reverse your "nice guy" style and become aloof or too hard to get and ignore her, thinking that you will be scoring points. If you adopt that strategy, you will be disqualified as someone not interested in purchasing the commodity. A qualified bidder shows interest and pursues the deal while remaining calm and collected. The window of opportunity comes with defined boundaries. A man must recognize the ceiling and the floor or face elimination. If the candidate man is too anxious he is out, and if he is too aloof he is out. The successful candidate needs to stay within the boundaries of her window's floor and ceiling in order to get her seal of approval and pass her screening process. A man must be nice enough to qualify as an interested candidate above the floor (minimum qualifications), and cool enough to stay below the ceiling (maximum qualifications). Stay within those boundaries and you will maximize your chances.

I once asked a guy who seemed to be very successful with women about his strategy. He said, "Every woman will give you a unique window of opportunity to pass through. If you are too timid, you are out, and if you are too aggressive, you are out. The challenge is to find the parameters of her specific window and stay within its boundaries." Too generous is out, and too stingy is out. If you are too generous, you are perceived as desperate and therefore disqualified. If you are too stingy, you are disqualified for lacking financial resources.

Too romantic is out, and too cold is out. If you are too romantic, you are perceived as needful. If you are too cold, you are perceived as beyond a woman's control.

Too kind is out, and too tough is out. If you are too kind, you are seen as weak and will be dumped in no time. Too tough is scary.

Too intelligent is a threat. Too stupid is embarrassing.

Too confident is arrogant, and too timid is a liability.

Too controlling is restricting, and too tolerant is weak.

Too authoritative is out, and too submissive is out. If you are too authoritative, you will make a woman nervous, and if you are too submissive she will see you as a pushover.

Too naïve is a turnoff, and too clever is a threat.

Too popular is out, and too unknown is out. If you are too popular, you are a headache, and if you are too unknown, you have no value.

Too daring is risky, and too shy is unmanly.

Too honest is boring, and too manipulative is tiring.

Too handsome is threatening, and too ugly is embarrassing.

Too intellectual is challenging, and too ignorant is unchallenging.

Too funny is lacking seriousness and accountability, and too serious is depressing.

The only exception to these boundaries is being too wealthy!

Women act as regulators, keeping men on their toes and

moderating their behavior. A window of opportunity is the screening process a woman uses before she welcomes a man into her life. A woman will give you a narrow window of opportunity to express yourself and to earn her seal of approval. That window has boundaries that are well defined in a woman's mind even if she isn't conscious of them. Think of this as a ceiling and a floor. If you exceed the ceiling or drop below the floor, you are out. You can pass only if you stay within the boundaries of this window. The floor is how much you like her, and the ceiling is how much you need her. To pass the floor test, your actions must make her feel that you like her. To pass the ceiling test, your actions must show that you are not desperate and can do without her.

A woman knows when you like her. Your actions will be sufficient indication. With her sharp sixth sense, a little liking goes long way. You do not have to scream it in her face or write it on the wall. To grant her approval, she also needs to know how well you can do without her. This takes her a longer time to determine. Your job is to make it clear to her, sooner rather than later, that you certainly can do without her. The longer it takes you to convey this message the longer it takes her to offer final approval. Let your actions say that you like her but that you can do without her. You don't have to play hard to get to make your point. If you play hard to get, you may get nothing. This behavior could identify you as one who is not interested and disqualifies you. On the other hand, you don't have to beg for her approval. This might send the wrong message, implying that you can't do without her and violating the ceiling boundary.

The size of the window varies from woman to woman, depending on the law of supply and demand. An attractive woman who gets a lot of attention is more likely to narrow her window than a less fortunate woman. A woman who experiences a lot of liking from men doesn't need any more confirmation. A small hint will do. She might be looking for confirmation of how well you can do without her. That explains why attractive women are harder to get and more likely to give their admirers a hard time than less attractive women. An attractive woman is harder to get because it is hard for her to encounter a man who does not want her. She must narrow the boundaries of her screening window to limit the number of candidates. In doing so, she becomes harder to get than an ordinary woman.

Why women are moderators is a question requiring more research within the commodity-market theory. Since moderating the consumer is what this question is about, it seems that a commodity-minded woman would rather moderate the consumer than moderate the market. That is because the market has too many variables and fluctuations, making it impossible to moderate. Continual adjustments and corrections are required to keep up with inevitable market changes involving fashion, trends, new concepts, education, friends, travels, etc. Having to deal with fluctuating market conditions in addition to a fluctuating consumer behavior would be a lot of moving targets to contend with. One of the two (consumer behavior or market behavior) must be controlled within defined parameters so that a woman can focus on accommodating a single set of moving targets. So a woman has no choice but to control the consumer.

3. Why would a woman give no attention to one guy while drooling over another?

Women's obsession with market value provides an easy answer to this question. A woman favors one guy over another because the favored one has something that would enhance her market value more than the other guy. That could be his car, his race, his looks, his fame, or the women around him. So the next time a woman becomes attached to you, don't think that you are a stud or God's gift to women. You simply have what it takes to make this particular woman feel a boost to her market value at the time she met you. You were the highest potential buyer available, at the time she met you and she chose you as bait to catch a bigger fish. If no higher bidder was found, she maintained the relationship. God only knows what you have to make her feel an inflated market value in clinging to you. The requirements vary from woman to woman and circumstance to circumstance, but market value remains the decisive factor. This fact does not diminish the glamour of love. It only redefines love in the mind of commodity-minded women as a rational conscious enterprise.

4. **Why does a commodity-minded woman want the man who *genuinely* does not want her?**

There are two answers for this question.

The first answer is; a woman wants a man who does not want her because she is afraid of taking responsibility for a man's dependence on her. If he loves her more than she loves him, she will be committed to an unwanted restriction. She is after the top bid and not after a specific character, and she will be restricted from pursuing higher goals under the pressure of his intense dependence. If a man does not love her intensely, she feels free to move forward without the risk of hurting him or being subject to his revenge. When a woman says, "I love this man," she actually means "I love the fact that he does not make me responsible for his feelings, and I love the freedom that he gives me to go about my business." And he is the highest bidder at the moment. That is what love means to the commodity-minded woman.

Controlling a man is both the goal and the momentum that keeps her interest in him alive. The irony is that the minute she achieves this goal, she loses interest in him. An experienced man will never give a woman full control over him. He will keep her at arm's length while holding bait in his hand to keep her pursuing him.

In developing a new relationship, one can take the commodity path or the romantic path. The commodity path is the one that those women prefer, because they are skilled at traveling it. The romantic path is the path of commitment, responsibility, morality, and all that stuff that scares these women and drives them away from men. If a woman is best at playing chess, why would she want to switch to backgammon... that she is not good at? An experienced man will play the game in her area of commodity interest, not his own, choosing a path far removed from romance. Furthermore, he will never grant her full control over his heart even after marriage. Taking the game to the romantic arena puts pressure on her to perform responsibly and rise to moral standards that she is not equipped to meet or willing to accommodate.

The second answer to the question "why does she want a man that does not want her?" The answer taken from the commodity market theoty is this: The goal of an auction is to find the highest bidder, and the one who bids last is the highest and most qualified candidate. In the world of relationships, a man's value is included in his overall bid, and he gains points by remaining hesitant to make a firm commitment. When he does this, a woman senses his higher value and is motivated to catch him.

5. **Why does a woman chase you when you push her away and dump you when you chase her? Why does she chase you until you show interest and then leave you? Why do anxious guys get dumped?**

When you push a woman away, you make her feel that you are better than she is. In commodity language, she feels that you have a higher market value than she does. Once she feels this way, you become a target for her to capture. Her goal is to bring you to your knees, which will automatically raise her market value above yours and give her the opportunity to brag to her competitors. Just remember the rule concerning the narrow window of opportunity she gives you. If you push her too hard, you are out, and if you go to the other extreme and beg her to stay with you, you are also out. You should be approachable but reserved, friendly but not inviting, interested but not anxious. The notion that hard-to-get men are interesting to women because they are a challenge is not a sufficient explanation. The real explanation is this. The hard-to-get man provides an opportunity for the woman to chase, capture, defeat, and dump, and consequently raise her market value above his. An easy-to-get man does not provide this opportunity. He will be wasting her time without adding to her market value.

6. Why do females use lame term of just wanting to be a friend instead of letting you know the real reason of not wanting to date you? Why not be honest to avoid him wanting more and not moving on?

I accidentally found this question on the Internet (http://wiki.answers.com/). What caught my attention was the answer posted by a female blogger named GossipGirl17. Here is what she said:

"Generally, that is the truth. They actually do want to be friends with you, and don't want to screw that up by going further. Other possibilities are:
–They like someone else.
–They really don't like you.
–Can't deal with a relationship currently.
If a girl says she wants to be just friends, take her word. Do your best to move on.
— GossipGirl17"

Her answer is intended to emphasize the moral aspect of this behavior but does not address other views like the commodity-mind point of view. From the commodity-mind theory, the behavior of keeping the man as a friend not as a lover is intended to keep as many men as possible around her to create the illusion of false demand that would enhance her image in the market. By leading a man on thinking that he can at least be a friend, she gives him the false hope that someday he could become the man of her choice.

Here are some other ways of saying the same thing while keeping the man attached just enough to fill the role of a virtual bidder in the virtual auction she builds around herself.

–I really like you, but I am confused.

–I don't really know what I want.

–I love you as a person, but I am not in love with you as a man.

–If I had a sister, I would introduce her to you.

–I feel comfortable with you, but I can't feel romantic yet.

7. Why do women like men who are self-confident, aggressive, funny, and popular?

Giggling, laughing, and smiling are some of the tools a woman has in her marketing kit. If she hangs out with a serious man who talks only about politics or science, she will have no way to display her charming smile and veneer-coated teeth or shake her fluffy, shiny hair. When she is displaying herself before a group of bidders, say in a nightclub or a singles bar, she would rather be talking, laughing, and looking happy. With a funny guy, she has a better chance of displaying her full bubbly capacity while pursuing her marketing campaign. Marilyn Monroe once said, "If you can make a woman laugh, you can make her do anything."

Furthermore, the attributes of self-confidence, aggressive and humorous belong to a guy with a high market value. When a woman describes her dream man as such, she is actually describing her standards of value. Instead of being obvious about her material standards for judging a man, she resorts to describing the attributes of power. Girls also like daring, crazy boys. They are rare and seen by women as valuable commodities. Women know by instinct that rare means expensive; according to the market law of supply and demand, the less the supply the higher the value. Women who think of themselves as commodities think that everybody else is a commodity. That includes men, who don't necessarily see themselves that way.

8. Why is she always agitating problems and provoking arguments with or without a reason?

In 2010 I heard about a group of women activists who claim that women have a right to stay home and stop working. This group complains that a new breed of young men take it for granted that a woman's position is behind a desk. What exactly do they want? Is this a reverse rebellion? Do they really feel this way and believe they have a case? I don't think so. Those women will always rebel against the current conditions, whatever they are. If you ask a woman like this to stay home, she rebels and wants to work. If you ask her to share in household expenses, she tells you, "My money is my money, and your money is my money." If you tell her she is expected to work and contribute to the partnership, she claims that she should stay home and that a real man would work and support her while she is busy bringing up the children. Her only aim is troublemaking. No matter what you do, she will find a way to disrupt peace and cause problems and arguments.

Why do they do this? Why can't they settle for peace and accept it as a way of life? The answer lies in exploring how a commodity item would feel, think, and behave under similar conditions. Peace in human relations, translated to commodity-market language, becomes recession, stagnation, and sluggish trade. In a good market, there are lots of buyers, vendors, commodities, deliveries, competition, noise, finance, banking, shopping, bargains, sales and lots of action. When recession hits, all this excitement disappears and the market comes to a halt.

How boring for a commodity to sit on the shelf day after day, week after week, season after season, without knowing where it stands in terms of market value!

A commodity-minded woman will feel similarly bored under peaceful conditions. She will ask herself, consciously or unconsciously, *where do I stand? Am I getting fat? Am I getting old? Is there a new wave of young girls out there creating a new market trend that I can't compete with? Is there a new fad that I am missing? What is my current market value?* Peace and stagnation in a relationship irritate her, leading her to create arguments and spark friction. This is also an easy way to assert her power and to test her market value in the eyes of the beholder. It is like a price check. If her man still meets her demands and surrenders to her wishes, then her market value remains the same. If he shows resentment or develops a negative attitude in response to hers, then she must check her weight, have a face-lift, or find out if he is dating a younger woman. If he is more conciliatory than ever, expressing regret and showering her with gifts while dining and wining her, then it is time for her to move on and find a better man! By making conciliatory measures, he is revealing an increase in her market value as compared with his. This could lead her to dump him and go after a higher bidder who will keep up with her newly raised value. If you ask the guy who got dumped, he will pathetically say, "Despite everything I did for her, she dumped me. I don't know why!" To him I say, **it is not despite, it is because.** Had he maintained his relative value higher than hers, she would have happily stayed with him knowing that he was the man.

An experienced man sense when friction is due. He knows when stagnation has arrived, peace has ended, and the truce has expired. His inner alarm signals danger, urging him to make a preemptive move. Before she creates a problem or demands an action, he strikes first, providing her with the excitement she needs while returning her to her proper position. This move assures the woman of her market value and confirms that his value is still higher. As soon as she is assured of where she stands in the market, she calms down and peace returns to the relationship. It is sad but true. A preemptive strike allows you to fight the inevitable battle on the ground of your choice. Instead of fighting about that other woman who flirted with you at the party, you can fight about missing your favorite tie. This won't cost you much and will give her the pleasure of creating friction; you will also assure her of her market value. What a puzzling creature she is!

Because she wants a man who does not want her, a hint of rejection by a man can actually make her happy. In order for her to know that he does not want her and become motivated to chase him, she needs to suffer his rejection. This suffering assures her that she is pursuing a good deal that will boost her market value. If she succeeds, she feels that she has gotten the best offer she can get for her assets. She will then brag about how he did not want her in the first place, but she got him in the end. Men do not behave the same way. If a man gets rejected, he moves on to other prospects in hopes that he will find the best match, not the best catch.

9. **She brags about how difficult it was to hunt and capture her man. Why?**

A married man introduced his beautiful wife to me at a Christmas party a few years ago. She told me that her husband at first had not wanted to marry her in the first place. No matter what she did, he still would not yield. It was not until she chased him down that he finally was convinced. What is interesting is that over several years she told me this story at least five times and made a deliberate effort to tell all her friends and coworkers that her husband was not an easy catch and had initially rejected the idea of marrying her. I wondered why she would brag that he had once dismissed the possibility of marriage. Wouldn't that lower her value and make her look cheap and desperate? I used the commodity-market metaphor to figure out the situation.

In a typical auction, there are low bidders, high bidders, and non-bidders. Low bidders get in and out quickly. Non bidders are there to watch the event like spectators at a baseball game. High bidders are those who look interested but will wait until the price goes high enough before revealing their interest, refusing to bid prematurely lest they increase the demand and therefore raise the price. Auctioneers know by experience who will turn out to be a low bidder, a non-bidder, or a high bidder. A high bidder is interested but hesitant. He hesitates because he is serious about buying an item. A low bidder does not hesitate. A high bidder understands the value of the item and therefore waits long enough to have it reach its highest potential before he shows his intentions. Similarly, a high-end man is interested but hesitant to make a commitment to a woman. That's because he is serious about her and he recognizes her value. If he had no interest in her, he would disappear from her sight and never return. A low-end man shows an early interest in hopes of getting a good deal or being released to move on to the next prospect.

The shrewd woman with her well-known sixth sense can detect the high-end guy. She knows that having him will add to her value. By declaring to her community that he initially rejected her, she is actually saying that he is the best she can attract and that no higher bidders exist for her. She places her value at its peak by telling her friends that she got the best deal and maxed out on her potential.

10. What constitutes a man's market value?

Wealth, 40 percent; popularity, 15 percent; physical appearance, 10 percent; personality, 10 percent; potential, 10 percent; education, 5 percent; family, 5 percent, race and age, 5 percent. Wealth is the liquid asset of market value. Popularity is a fixed asset of influence and political power. Physical appearance, size, color, and attractiveness contribute to success and could be translated into dollars. Personality and charisma are valuable for social influence. The remaining components are cosmetic incidentals that come in handy when the score is even between two candidates. Potential could apply to wealth, education, and popularity if the candidate plays his cards well. For example, if a guy is accepted to a school of medicine and is working as a janitor to finance his education, he will score high on potential and probably win the race against a candidate who has established a decent value but doesn't have as high an upside. That explains why some women will pick a neglected guy. They hope to nurture his potential growth and translate that into high market value. This guy is what I call a fixer upper; he does not cost much to catch but could bring a very high value when his potential comes to full fruition.

11. **Have you ever entertained a woman out to nice places, showered her with flowers and expensive gifts, and had her turn you down for someone else who didn't treat her half as well?**

If you have, then you are a nice guy and it is only normal for that to happen. When you do these foolish things, you send a clear message: "I don't think you'll like me for who I am, so I'm going to try to buy your attention and affection." Your good intentions usually come across to commodity-minded women as overcompensation for insecurity and lack of self-worth. In addition, your generosity could be perceived as a cheap attempt to manipulate her feelings.

Let's express this conclusion in mathematics for our fellow mathematicians. Knowing that she thinks like a commodity, she assumes that everyone else have the same mentality. She also knows her exact market value. Based on this knowledge, she uses the following formula to put a value on the man interested in her.

Her value = his value + the value of his offerings.

In this formula her value is constant because she knows it. If she perceives his value to be less than hers, she expects him to balance the equation with sufficient funds presented in gifts, trips, and other offerings. If he fails to do so, she will either leave him to find a better deal or make up for the difference in value by having other affair(s) to finance the gap. If there are no other bidders around her to finance the gap, she will make him pay for it in misery and friction. Once you know the rules, you can understand what is going on in her mind. A naïve man will keep on giving, hoping that she will give him credit for being so generous. But she will think she has earned everything that he gives. She will believe that she has received these gifts solely because of herself. She will give no credit to the giver.

Now let's go back to the formula. Since this woman knows her value (or lack of it) very well, balancing the formula by adding more gifts can only reduce the giver's value. So, while he gives, hoping to get high marks for his generosity, he finds himself reduced and then ditched. This is the kind of guy who will tell me, "Despite everything I did for her, she dumped me." And I will reply, "This happened not despite what you did, but because of it." At least now it will no longer be a puzzle when you get dumped for good behavior! No good deed will go unpunished. I can go on and on forever with examples of nice guys who acted as perfect gentlemen, then paid the price for it, but I am sure you have your own collection of memories. I once used this knowledge to get rid of a gal without hurting her feelings. To avoid her fury and revenge, I wanted her to take the lead in terminating the relationship. So I sent her an expensive gift for Valentine's Day after which she stopped calling me. When she called me ten months later to resume the relationship, I was already in a new one and apologized to her.

The reverse of this tactic is also true. Knocking down a commodity woman once in a while will trigger the mathematical formula in her mind and make her feel your relatively higher value. Then it becomes her job to balance the equation by showing good behavior.

A commodity-minded woman is fair. If she perceives her man's value to be much higher than hers, she becomes more willing to finance the difference in gifts, loans, attention, and sex. Experienced men and playboys seem to know about this mathematical formula and take advantage of it by faking a higher market value, fooling the lady into financing their companionship and showering them with gifts and favors. This also explains why some women with low self-esteem support their lovers and put up with their abuse. It seems that everybody is doing whatever it takes to balance the equation and get the math right. After all, in balance there is stability.

Black hole: the link between sex and astronomy

In science, a black hole is a star that exceeded the maximum size a star can take. There is a critical balance between size and gravity that if exceeded, the star collapses on itself due to an enormous gravitational force that attracts anything coming near it—including its own matter and passing light.

What does this have to do with women? Well, some women have a greater power of attraction than one man can afford. Such a woman cannot have just one man courting her. She needs to have several men contributing to provide for her well-being and to display her high value. This is what

I call a black hole woman since by exceeding the normal limit of attractiveness; she ends up pulling in anything that comes near her.

Show me the money

Would you ever tell a vendor that you love his product but don't have enough money to buy it and then expect him to pledge it to you? Of course not. He would think you are out of your mind. You will draw the same reaction if you tell a woman that you love her, complain about your financial condition, and then expect her to remain with you! The best she will do is give you the cold shoulder, thank you for being honest and saving her time, then move on to the next guy. Experienced men know how to flash symbols of power and display a high market value that gets the job done quickly and easily. They get a glass of milk without having to buy the cow.

When Commodity Women Socialize

12. **Why do you get more attention from women when you are already in a relationship or when you are accompanied by an attractive woman?**

Some would say that when you are involved in a relationship you are more relaxed and satisfied and therefore attractive. Nonsense. Others would say that having a lot of women around you implies that you have something of value that is worth pursuing. More nonsense.

In fact, it has nothing to do with you. These women are in competition with each other and you happened to be in the middle of it. If you dive into Shark Lake holding a piece of fresh meat, sharks will be all over you. If you let go of the meat, they will leave you alone. You are only serving as a trophy, helping the winning woman claim the highest market value over her competitors. Shortly after declaring victory over her competitors, she will move up the ladder in pursuit of a better man with a higher market value than yours, and so on. At the end of the auction, when no higher bidders are available, she will realize that she has achieved her highest potential and gotten the best offer. She will hold on to this offer, awaiting a higher one. If you examine a photo album of her ex-boyfriends, you will see an incremental increase in their values. You might also be assured that your value is the highest of all so far. Such a relationship is based on best available offer rather than greatest compatibility.

The Bachelor TV reality show is a good illustration of women competing based on their market value. Twenty women are selected to compete for the heart of one man, who will supposedly marry the winner. Watching the reactions of the nineteen who fall short, you can tell that their responses have nothing to do with loving the man or marrying him. Some of them break into tears. One had a nervous breakdown. Some of them criticize the winner or criticize each other. The competition is all about establishing market value. The winner proves that she has the highest market value and will brag about it for the rest of her life. She will probably stay married to the bachelor for few months and then forget about him. But she will never forget that she won against nineteen other beautiful women. This is the real trophy that she will carry with her to the grave. Her delight has nothing to do with the man. He could have been a robot, and these contestants would have acted the same way.

13. Why is she friendlier with strangers while in the company of her man?

I am especially cautious when I get an uninvited smile or receive unexpected eye contact from an attractive female stranger sitting alone in a nightclub or a coffee shop. If something looks too good to be true, it probably is. I usually wait a few minutes before I react, only to find her man returning from the bathroom or a phone call. Then I ask myself, *Why is she acting like this, since her man stepped away for a few minutes? Is she looking for an upgrade or just becoming friendly all of a sudden?*

I took this question to the commodity market and soon enough I found the answer. In order for her to assert her value in the eyes of her man she has to manipulate the market to her advantage. By creating false demand, her value goes up, according to the law of supply and demand. If she is negotiating a sponsorship deal with her man (as in marriage), her popularity in the market makes her look desirable and adds to her value. That happens only in her mind because her man does not necessarily think like a commodity as she does. He is probably after the best match, not the best catch. The next time you see a female stranger smiling at you for no apparent reason, ask yourself, *Am I really that likable, or is she just attempting to get a reaction from me to score in front of her man?* There is no need to be paranoid; it is just nice to know what you are dealing with and where you stand. Most guys would rather take credit for their ability to score, and they tend to explain things in terms of their egos.

A guy once told me that he got dates for hire at a karaoke bar. "A girl wouldn't go with anybody, though. She ought to like you first," he proudly explained. So many women cash in by playing on the need for self-assurance that this guy showed. This is known as catering to men's egos.

14. Why does she have a sixth sense?

Evolution is fair. It would not take something away from you unless it gave you an equal or better deal. Throughout history, men have possessed a lot of power over women, controlling their moves and keeping them in the cave. Women had plenty of time while *caving around* to stay focused and develop an inner strength that took the shape of intuition and sixth-sense skills. Any woman has the ability to feel minute changes in her man's body language and to read his mind. An experienced man knows how to block her sixth-sense antenna and dissipate her detection abilities. Those men can even use women's power of intuition to their advantage by sending misleading information and turning women's antennae the opposite way. To sharpen such a skill, we first need to understand how it works. I am still researching this issue. If you find out how it works let me know!

15. Why do men and women have different opinions about fashion shows or strip bars of corresponding sex?

Women activists are always annoyed by fashion shows displaying beautiful female models. But we never hear about men objecting to male models or to athletes showing off their muscles. Why do men and women respond differently in these cases? I took the question to the commodity market in search for an answer, and here it is. When a commodity-minded woman is faced with commercial showing competitors with higher value than hers, she protests the display. She knows that exposing buyers to commodities of higher value will educate the buyers and refine their taste. An inferior commodity would rather have buyers stay naïve and think highly of her than compare her with the high end of the market and find out what other commodities have to offer. On the other hand, since men don't think of themselves as commodities but rather as individuals looking for the best match in a relationship, they do not care about what other guys have to offer. If other guys make a better match, so be it. A man will just keep looking in the market for the best match he can find, not the best offer. Of course some guys will look for the best commodity they can afford, but that will not yield a long-term relationship. It will just be good enough for a quick fix.

16. Why will a woman lead on several guys when she is not interested in any of them?

In a television interview, several female nightclub goers agreed that they like aggressive guys who take the lead in approaching them. When they were asked to explain, one of them said that she likes a guy who comes to her instead of sitting alone staring at her or waiting for her to make the first move. She also said that she would never strike up a conversation with a man. So while she was encouraging forward behavior by men, she declined to make similar moves toward them. She gave a dismissive wave of her hand as if to say, "I am too good to take the initiative or approach a guy." But if she thought it was degrading to make the first move, why did she like guys who took the initiative? Wasn't that a double standard?

No, it was not. Such a woman makes a clear distinction between her role as a commodity and a guy's role as a consumer. Obviously, a commodity would like to have a crowd of buyers around her, checking her out, approaching her, and asking questions about the package and the price. That adds to her value, creating a false demand that increases her market value through the law of supply and demand. For the same reason, when she wants to attract a specific man, she tries to surround herself with as many men as possible to increase her value in his eyes and get his attention. She does this because she mistakenly thinks that men have the same mentality as she does concerning commodity competition. She thinks that men will compete with each other (like women compete with each other) to have her. How little she knows! Instead of attracting them, this behavior discourages a lot of men and makes them feel that she is a butterfly, not a safe bet.

One female nightclub goer said, "If I sit next to a guy at the bar, he'd better pay for my drinks because if he does not, the guy on the other side will."

17. Why do women always go for men they cannot have, and reject single guys when they ask them out?

I copied this question from the Internet, and I leave it to the reader to provide his own answer. Here is one response.

"I might go to a club or something and see women hitting on the DJ(s), the bouncers, or the bartenders who are there to collect a check, but they always ignore the guys who are in the club to see them.

I was also in college where there was a girl that was from out of state who did not know anybody, I tried to ask her out one Friday night, and she turned me down saying she had a man, the next day my friend told me this chick was trying to ask him out, but he turned her down because he has a woman already, come to find out it was the same girl who I had asked out the night before (which was awkward), I also look way better than my friend does, I am six foot two, 190 pounds, and he is a chubby five foot ten, 240 pounds.

"Now here we are. Both me and that new girl sit in our dorms twiddling our thumbs on a Saturday night with nothing to do. What is the matter with you women? Damn!"

18. Why are nightclubs the most difficult places to pick up a date?

Nightclubs are known as meat markets, places where you "meet" lots of women. Unfortunately, most of those women are unhappy and bored with their lives. They are trying to find temporary pain relief and instant fun. Their self-esteem has hit rock bottom or is at least flagging. They feel less valuable or even fear that they have become worthless. Unable to compete in the ordinary market, they go to the discount market of nightclubs to display their assets and make a quick sale.

Yes, nightclubs are the market for discounted commodities. A woman battling negative feelings about herself is looking for Mr. Right to affirm her value in front of her competitors and raise it to where she believes it should be. She will ignore an average, humble-looking guy lest she be seen with him and reveal the low self-worth she is trying to hide. Due to her low self-esteem, she is sensitive to interactions that might magnify her feelings and make them public. Because this woman sees her market value as her most important asset, she would rather dance with her girlfriends and keep her value anonymous than associate with a guy who would confirm her discounted status.

Poor guys, they go to these clubs full of hope and ambition only to find a bunch of discounted commodities trying to climb onto Mr. Right's shoulders if he ever appears. To get past their defensive attitude and avoid their radar, I devised a new way of interacting with women in clubs. I usually arrive with a guy more handsome than I am. We search until we find two targets. He goes first, approaching the one who apparently has lower market value. In most cases, she immediately accepts his invitation, leaving her more expensive friend wondering what is wrong with her. While she is out of balance, I approach the temporarily shaken princess and spare her from defeat and misery by asking her to dance. Since her price has been unexpectedly compromised by having a handsome guy choose her ugly friend over her, she is eager to cooperate with anyone who will save her the embarrassment of being the second choice. No one will notice whether she was taken first or second if she leaves her seat quickly and hides among the dancing crowd.

Had I asked the beautiful woman first, she wouldn't have given me the time of day, anticipating a better offer from a higher-value dude. I call my approach the back-door attack because it is designed to provoke the woman into protecting her current value instead of aspiring for a higher one. This tactic works. Give it a try.

Nightclubs are among the most difficult places to pick up a date because women are engaged in fierce competition and are acutely aware of their value. Beaches and gymnasiums are second and third in difficulty; these are the spots where women do maintenance work, tanning and trimming their bodies before parading them in the meat market.

Where are the easy places to catch a date? These are the places where commodity-minded women least expect an attack and therefore let their guard down and turn off their sixth-sense radar. These places include funeral homes, dental clinics, pet shops, IRS offices, bus stops, state unemployment offices, airplanes, seminar rooms, and grocery stores.

Patterns of Behavior

19. She doesn't know what she wants. She only knows what she doesn't want. Why?

First of all, is it true that she doesn't know what she wants? Or is she too ashamed to say, "I am looking for the highest bidder, and I don't care what other qualities he has"?

Knowing what she does not want means that she can only choose by eliminating unqualified candidates one at a time until the highest bidder remains. She chooses by rule of omission not by rule of commission, like the case of an auction.

Knowing what one wants is the mindset of a buyer, not a seller. A Buyer is looking for a predefined item that best suit his needs, while a seller is looking for the highest offer he can get for the item he sells. Let's switch to our commodity market metaphor and find the parallel answer. The buyer goes to an auction knowing with a high degree of certainty what he is looking for. A seller, on the other hand, has no specific criteria about the buyer other than looking for the highest bidder with enough cash.

In an auction, everyone acknowledges that the highest bidder will get the item for sale. However, in a relationship, a man wants a woman who will be loyal to him, not to his wallet. Therefore, it is difficult for a woman to admit that her loyalty is to his wallet, not to him. She will lose the sale if she reveals her true intentions. She will safely reveal what she does not want, but she would not admit what she wants.

20. Why does she say that she wants one thing when she really wants another?

She doesn't know what she wants. She does not seem to make up her mind easily as if her judging criteria fluctuate depending on time and circumstance. In addition to the emotional decision making process, what she likes is totally different from what she gets attached to. She likes what she needs as a human being; compassion, moral support, love, belonging, appreciation. She gets attached to those things involving the marketability of her assets. Confusion arises when the dividing line between commodity interest and human interest is not clear.

A shrewd man should be able to distinguish between what the commodity mind desires and what the human spirit needs. Next time you hear her say, "I really like the man who holds my purse and open doors for me," ask yourself whether she likes having you do these things because she appreciates a man who displays care and respect for his woman or because you have enhanced her market value in public. Some women have dual personalities when it comes to dealing with guys—one as a human being and another as a commodity. So before you give her what she says she wants, make sure you understand which of her personalities is speaking to you. I promise that you will never be confused again.

21. Why would a woman say she is happily married when she is really searching for an attorney to get a divorce?

A happily married man is quite an attraction for a woman to pursue since he comes with a wife whom he loves, for her to compete with. He is not sexually or emotionally needy, which makes him an expensive catch. If she can induce him to cheat on his wife, then she earns a market value higher than hers and the bonus of turning his happy marriage into a miserable one. Similarly, a woman on the hunt may think that if she claims to be happily married she will get guys to pursue her. She does not know that men and women have different mind-sets.

On the other hand, when a man tells a woman that he is getting divorced, his chances of dating her are no better than his chances of winning the lottery. That is because she feels his need for moral support and dependence, and would detract from his value in her eyes. Her mission is to go after value. "Who needs that?" she thinks. Who wants a guy who is not wanted by another woman? Who wants a guy who comes without a woman so she can compete with her and win? *"A stand-alone guy? Naaa. How miserable!"* she thinks. Similarly, when she is going through a divorce, she overreacts in hiding it from potential dates by telling them that she is happily married. Again, she does this because she mistakenly thinks that men have the same mentality as women do. The next time you hear a woman say that she is happily married, ask her out. She is available.

22. Why would she deliberately reveal her relationship with a married or committed man? But he does not do the same?

Capturing a married or committed man raises a woman's market value above that of his wife. If his wife is beautiful and known to have a high market value, the intruding woman will automatically place her value above the betrayed wife's. Why do you think Monica Lewinsky revealed her affair with Bill Clinton through a friend? As for men, market value is not an issue for them. He keeps the relationship confidential so he can enjoy it longer.

Catching a single man has a different flavor. A single man is supposedly more needful of sex and affection than a married man. Therefore, catching a married man implies a greater power of attraction than catching a single man. This adds to a woman's market value in relation to her competitors.

23. Why does a housewife attempt to possess her children?

Traditionally, while the father works hard to provide for the household, the mother spends time with the children and does chores at home. Thus she asserts her control over the children and eventually guarantees that they will be loyal to her rather than sharing loyalty equally with the father. While the husband is busy securing the present and the future, the wife is busy recruiting the children to her side. You see the outcome of this strategy when a couple decides to divorce. The children will most likely side with the mother and support her against their father. Had the father been alerted to the potential recruitment of his children against him, he would have bolstered his presence in the home and made sure their loyalty was evenly shared.

I saw an interesting report on TV about a husband who ended up staying home while his wife worked and provided for the household. Despite the husband's devotion and full-time housekeeping efforts, the children never quit calling their mother at work and she never stopped returning their calls and giving them directions on what to do. She managed the house remotely. She seemed to be helping the family, but in reality she was asserting her position, ensuring sufficient control and loyalty just in case.

Children's ownership and loyalty adds to a woman's market value. The net worth of a woman (as she would calculate it) is the sum of factors that fluctuate depending on market conditions. These factors include age, beauty, figure, elegance, personality, manners, voice pitch, a husband's

79

status and income, car model, house size and location, children's health and success, bank accounts, and jewelry, etc. The most important and least likely to fluctuate is children's success. Their success is her success. The more successful her children are, the higher her market value will be. The more she loses market value due to aging the more she emphasizes the value of her children. Sharing her children's success with her husband detracts from the market value associated with that success. She would rather take full credit for their success. This makes her more possessive of the children from an early age and more willing to invest time and effort in managing them and ensuring her control and their loyalty.

While on the topic of fluctuating market value, it is fair to say that the average woman is at the peak of her market value from ages nineteen to twenty-nine. In these ten critical years, a woman must act quickly to establish her future, landing a guy, bearing children, and sowing the seeds for later value that should offset any market decline that comes with aging. On the other hand, guys have from ages eighteen to sixty-five or more (seventy-five and up with Viagra) to fulfill their dreams and enjoy the fruits of their work. So women have ten years to plant and harvest the seeds of life, while men have at least fifty. That is a 400 percent greater chance of success. Men can screw up their lives and have more chances to get back on track than women do.

Whether Mother Nature is fair is not the point. Because women have such a short time to make an impact, their actions become crucial. The pressure put on women to perform and achieve makes them less sensitive to men's circumstances and swifter in determining whether a relationship is rewarding and will lead to long-term security. For commodity-minded women, love is not based on a foolish whim as it is for many men and a lot of innocent women.

24. Why does a woman insist on using exact change at the checkout counter, disregarding the long line behind her while searching for two pennies and a dime in her wallet? Most men do not do that.

Here is how the question was posted online.

"Why do women always pay with exact change? I never see a guy pay with exact change."

These are some of the answers, with no mention of gender.

—"Post office, turnpike booth, grocery store ... counting pennies and delaying everything! I wonder if they think they are 'saving' money or something ... I never see a guy pay with exact change."

— "Guys don't carry change because it sounds gay if you walk with a jingle."

— "Because it's cute? Usually it is old women holding up the line!"

— "I suspect it's more about why men don't pay with exact change! Most-o-my-buds ain't so good at ciphering."

— "What else are you supposed to do with it?"

—"Because they are smarter than us!"

— "They got all that shit in the purse; might as well make use of it."

Now let's try to apply the commodity market theory to find an answer to this question. The normal behavior is to pay with whatever money you have and leave the line quickly so people behind you can go about their business.

Later on you take the change you received and place it in a jar. When the jar is full, you take the coins to a change machine or to a bank and get some bills for them. So no money is saved or lost.

So why do women pay with exact change if there is no savings or loss? The unusable capital in a jar full of coins will eventually be regained. For men, this pending cash is savings to use when they run out of money. For women, change is idle capital that should be used immediately to bring about instant gratification. Commodity-minded women prefer instant gratification over delayed gratification. Isn't that what a commodity item likes too? When you buy a commodity in the market, the small business owner would rather get paid in cash than get paid with credit. This allows him to manage his small business better and know his exact net worth at the end of each day. A commodity-minded woman needs to know at all times how much she has in liquid assets (cash) and what her net worth is.

25. Why do women always complain about men rushing them into a relationship while men do not have similar complaint?

When you apply for a job or a loan, a potential employer or lender will need time to verify your references, history, and credit report before committing to a long-term relationship. This verification and credit check typically take only a short while because the information is usually well documented and readily available. Similarly, a commodity-minded woman needs time to verify your assets, job, annual income, and debt before she gets too intimate with you. The sooner you provide her with this information the sooner she opens up and gives you the green light to commence the relationship. Any attempt by the man to speed things up before releasing this information will be labeled as "rushing the relationship."

Sometimes the woman will give the man hints like, "I don't know you well enough" or "We just met and I need more time to know you" or "I am really confused and need to understand myself better" or "I don't know what I want; I only know what I don't want."

A woman will also slow down the development of a relationship to protect it against the countdown for termination. Slowing the pace and delaying the starting point of sexual intimacy will stretch the relationship's shelf life.

Men (the consumers) do not need to verify anything about the woman except the desirability of her body—

the very thing she is holding back until she completes her investigation.

Attitude

26. Hell has no fury like a woman scorned. Why?

The worst thing you can do to a woman is to undermine her market value in public or in front of another woman. One way to do this is by cheating on her with a woman of lesser market value. If you want to see a demonstration, favor a woman of lesser market value over her. In doing so, you will unleash her fury in many forms and directions. Experienced men know exactly what I mean and realize that unleashing this power could have a devastating effect on their lives.

The good news is that favoring another woman with higher market value is not as bad and might not produce full dose of retaliation. That is because it gives your woman the opportunity to compete with a woman of higher price tag with a good chance of raising her value if she wins the battle. She is challenged to do whatever it takes to bring you back. Then she can brag about her victory. She can also declare her upgraded market value by telling the story to the world. She will accept competition with a woman of higher value because there is no risk of losing her own market value to a higher woman. If she loses the battle, she escapes with her market value intact. If she wins, her value will soar above that of her competitor. On the other hand, if she defeats an inferior competitor, she has nothing to gain; her market value will remain the same. But if she loses, her value will sink below her inferior competitor's, and she will unleash her fury as she sinks. Think of the sinking of the *Titanic*. You don't want to see it except on the big screen.

Look at male celebrities' affairs and how their women react when the news breaks. If the betrayed woman is more beautiful than the intruding woman, she asks for a divorce. If the betrayed woman is less attractive than the intruding woman, she fights tooth and nail to keep her man.

Another way to unleash your woman's fury is to dump her. When you do that, you are dropping her market value below yours, and she will attempt to get back at you with creative plans for retaliation. The best way to end a relationship peacefully is to make her feel that this was her decision. That way you avoid her fury. Men don't worry about market value issues. They have egos that get in their way only when they deal with each other.

27. Why do commodity-minded women play hard to get?

Market conditions and a woman's personality determine whether she plays hard to get. If the demand is higher than the supply of commodities, then it is a sellers' market and the price goes up. In this environment, women adopt a hard-to-get attitude. If the demand decreases or the supply rises, commodities go on sale, and this can produce surprising changes in behavior. Playing hard to get is like holding a price tag that says, "I am expensive. Come and get it if you can afford me."

The situation varies from market to market depending solely on the law of supply and demand. For an average guy, the chance of getting a good deal in one city could be much higher than in another city. Getting a good deal in San Francisco would probably cost him an arm and leg due to the dominant gay community and the relative scarcity of heterosexual women.

Physical appearance could also contribute to a hard-to-get attitude in *some* women. For example, you can tell the difference between women with breast implants and women with naturally large breasts by the attitudes of these women. Naturally large-breasted women as teens were exposed to unwelcomed attention before they were prepared to deal with it. They learned to say no at an early age, when yes was not even an option. By age twenty-five when they are at the peak of their blooming sexuality, they already have ten years of solid "no" experience that shows in the way they carry themselves and handle their relationships. Their body language will say, "No. I am hard to get."

28. When you give her leverage she uses it against you. Why?

A woman who feels, thinks, and acts as a commodity will interpret the world around her according to a commodity value system. She believes that everything she receives is in return for a service she provides. She cannot understand why a man would give her something unless he expects something in return. She cannot see the kindness behind giving. If she receives some favor or gift, she takes credit for it, thinking she earned it. The giver, she believes, is repaying a debt he owed her or is expecting something in return. In either case, she attributes his kindness not to his good nature or his morality but to her ability to earn it. Remember the girl chatting in the gym about being wined and dined without paying a penny? She boasted of her ability to earn the treat, making no reference to the generosity of her host.

When a man extends leverage to his woman, she feels that she has earned it, interpreting it as a reward for being in the relationship. If a man tells his woman to feel free to use his credit card, she believes that the sky is the limit and uses that leverage until the credit card is maxed out. If he tells her not to worry about housekeeping and to leave the work for him, she will use this leverage to the full extent and even have him wash her car too.

When you offer leverage to a woman, she may not only use it to the full extent but use it against you. I dated a woman for a few months, paying for her groceries and casual shopping as a matter of courtesy. A few weeks into the relationship, she presented me with her housing lease, anticipating that I would pay her rent. Another woman gave me her credit card bills, claiming to have maxed out her line of credit, before we even got in a serious relationship.

Commodity-minded women are rebels, and rebels like to cross the line, no matter how near or far the line is. You might as well give her a nearby line to enjoy crossing it causing no harm and fulfill her inevitable rebelling agenda. For instance, if you are willing to grant her a week out of town to visit her folks, start the negotiations at four days only and barely tolerate her crossing this boundary, eventually settling on the week. This strategy is closely related to negotiation tactics in the commodity market. In a market that allows price negotiations, the seller raises the price a small percentage over the value he desires to give the buyer room to haggle and get the sense of winning. On the other hand, the buyer will drop the price below the value he would settle for, expecting to meet the seller halfway. In the end, buyer and seller will close the deal happily, enjoying a false sense of victory. To trigger negotiations, buyers are taught to shriek at any price quoted by the seller. This tactic is similar to dropping a week of vacation down to four days to give room for negotiations and end up with the result you want. Accepting one week will yield two. Accepting two weeks will produce three. Accepting a month will mean two. That's because a woman must cross the boundary you establish in order to get the feeling that she has won. You might as well give her that feeling at an affordable price you can pay.

Freedom's boundaries

On a similar social issue, let's examine freedom boundaries in a given society. Even freedom needs well-defined boundaries in order to guard it against rebels, while allowing them to cross these boundaries. Rebels will search for the current state of acceptable boundaries and make a deliberate effort to break them and cross the line. It's the nature of rebellion. This is what rebels do, crossing lines. When legislators shift the boundaries of freedom from point A to point B, rebels will cross over to point C. Then a few years later, legislators will succumb to the rebels' pressure and shift the boundaries to point C, only to encounter a new generation of rebels crossing the line toward point D. The process will continue until the entire society reaches point Z, a point of no return, and risks suicide at the edge of a cliff.

We cannot climb indefinitely. There must be a logical point where climbing ends with a fence to guard us. Empires collapse when they reach that point of no return and find no guarding fence preventing them from falling off of the cliff.

29. Why does reverse psychology work well with women? Why does she like to do the opposite of what you want?

She feels that your gain is her loss, so she tries to prevent it from happening. But why does she feel this way? What is it in the commodity market that makes a commodity oppose the wishes of her prospective buyers? This is a bargaining tactic intended to make you feel that you owe her more for getting your way. For example, if you want to go to the movies and she quickly agrees to go, you might think that you are giving her a treat and that she now owes you something. But if she objects, resists the plan, then barely accepts it, you owe her for getting your way. So she is cashing in on your desire to go to the movies, hoping to double dip by attending and also getting bonus for escorting you. There is no such a thing as a free ride.

In sales negotiations, when your opponent finally offers the price that you like, your initial reluctance to accept it will assure him that the price is right. This will assure the opponent that he has won and he will happily close the deal. In the same way, a woman assures you that you got a good deal by taking her to the movies. Now you owe her something.

30. Why won't she give him what he wants until he shows signs of giving up?

A woman holds back, hoping that her admirer will show his hand first. She wants to know how desperate he is. The more desperate he is, the longer he will wait and the more she will hold back. By doing this, she also shows that she does not come cheap, increasing her market value. A man will give up when he has done all he can, reached the end of his rope, and is ready to move on to another relationship that will fulfill his sexual and emotional needs. A woman's response time to his needs varies from man to man, depending on how soon he shows signs of giving up. From the commodity-mind vantage point, giving up is an indication of reaching the maximum possible gain she can get after which it will start to decline. When the man runs out of patience, she becomes more receptive and is willing to make concessions to reach a compromise.

31. Why would a woman choose the worst time to break up with you—when you are most vulnerable and most need her companionship and moral support?

Hitting bottom by losing your job, filing for bankruptcy, receiving a sentence in jail, losing your house in foreclosure, or becoming severely ill, losing your throne as a king, etc. are all examples of circumstances that would lead your woman to break up with you when you are most needful to her presence and support. How could she do that and face herself and the world honorably? Here is how. For the commodity-minded woman, losing market value is the most unethical and degrading act a commodity can tolerate and harm her image. Since she thinks that everybody has a mind like hers, she assumes that everybody will understand that losing market value is unethical act that deserves to be punished. Thus she is justified in deserting you. She believes that maintaining a high value and working hard to remain on top are expressions of love and commitment. If you really loved her, you would never have allowed circumstances to drag you so low.

Thanks to this mind-set, humanity has been progressively on the rise, striving to prosper and continually struggling against the forces that lead to decline or reduction in market value. The main difference between our species and others is our ability to progress by competing with each other. This accounts for our rapid rise. Had we not been prompted to pursue this path, we would still be hunting for food and our civilization would never have arisen. We owe it to the commodity mind-set that created a momentum that never weakened and has led to humanity's growth and maturity.

In the world of finance, lenders will offer you loans when you don't need one. They will deny you a loan when you most need it. Reading a book about financing real estate projects, I learnt that lenders tend to offer loans to people who don't need them. Meanwhile, people who desperately need loans and do their best to get them will be disqualified and denied the loan. There are similarities between this situation and the attitude of many women toward relationships. Men who are least interested in a relationship will get lots of offers, while those who try the hardest will be placed on the back burner or totally ignored. Well, it sounds that we found another link to the commodity market metaphor. The explanation can be found in the world of finance. Lenders prefer to give their money to people who already have plenty of it, reducing the risk and providing a business relationship they can rely on. Similarly, women prefer to enter a relationship with a man who has lots of them. In doing so, she reduces the risk of taking on a man who will be dependent on her while hoping she could depend on him.

The same rule applies to the employment market. In a competitive market, it is much easier to get a job when you already have one. Potential employers would rather hire you if you are already working; because your knowledge and momentum are current and you don't need time to get up to speed. In addition, you have an instant reference by being employed. Having a job also gives you more bargaining power as a job seeker. You can ask for equal or higher salary or benefits than what you now receive. As if being unemployed is not bad enough, the unemployed person doesn't even have first priority in seeking a job!

Performance

32. How can you get laid for free?

While men have only power to offer, women have a variety of assets to offer in addition to that. If you think you can get what they have for free, you are asking for trouble. You might choose to pay in cash, credit, favors, gifts, or lifetime sponsorship (as in marriage). If this list does not appeal to you, consider your career, your reputation, your peace of mind, your health, or even your life. Which list would you rather choose from? You are better off choosing your method of payment than having her choose it for you.

A commodity-minded woman believes that her contribution to a relationship is in sexual favors, period. Although she uses her sexuality for financial gain, she will never admit it.

I once asked a beautiful single lady in her mid-thirties about her ideal man for marriage. After thinking for a couple of seconds, she said, "One who is wealthy, with no less than $150,000 in income at my disposal, handsome, and younger than me with a PhD." Astonished for her candid requirements, I asked what she would contribute to the marriage to balance these enormous requirements. She looked at me in rage and said in a protesting tone, "My beauty, my passion, and my personality." Then she exploded at me. "How could you ask a woman such a question?" she shouted. "Isn't what I've got to offer already enough? Are you out of your mind?" She berated me for asking such a stupid question. I could not walk away to save face, because we were having dinner on a cruise ship in the middle of San Francisco Bay and the water was too cold to jump in! I did my best to calm her down, apologizing, offering more drinks and dessert, changing the subject, and even offering my jacket to keep her warm until she finally stopped yelling. After we left the boat, I gave her a ride home and wished her a good night. I never asked her out or wanted to see her again.

I paid the price for my question, but I learned my lesson: never ask a commodity-minded woman about her contribution to a relationship. She offers only one thing. When you ask such a question, you are either denying the value of what she offers, or you are asking for an additional contribution, or you are asking for trouble!

33. Early in a relationship, why does she resist sexual advances and deny her sexual needs? Why does she hide her sexual involvement behind love, being drunk, being raped or feeling lonely, but never attributes them to sexual need?

Here is how a commodity-minded woman perceives the world of relationships. If she is offering sex, then the man is the one who needs it. She doesn't. Or at least he needs it more than she does. In a relationship transaction, sexual need is a debt. If a man's penis represents a debt, then a woman's vagina is a credit. Therefore men should pay their debt while women should collect a credit. Most men don't mind showing their need. They just want to get laid. On the other hand, women prefer to hide their need or their despair to protect their market value from any debt. One woman told me that she once pretended to be a prostitute in order to have sex! If she is selling sex, she doesn't have to admit her need for it. Admitting a need for sex would compromise her market value and give the buyers (men) unnecessary bargaining power. This would be like a salesman telling a buyer that he must sell all the cars on the lot soon to make room for the new models. A buyer will take advantage of the situation and get a car at a bargain price.

Instead of trading love for love, need for need, body for body, and sex for sex, her strategy is to trade her body for a full sponsorship that will automatically grant her maximum return on her investment. On many occasions, a woman asks the man to buy her a drink in a nightclub or demands a dinner before she gets in the sack. The man thinks she is using him. In fact, she is hiding her sexual needs behind returning the man's favor. She makes him think that she is not needful but is simply rewarding him for his kindness.

Let's examine this transaction further. If having sex equals a hundred dollars and having dinner equals a hundred dollars, then she earned two hundred for having both. The man's account is not as rewarding. He gained a hundred dollars for sex but lost a hundred for dinner, ending up with nothing. What a deal! The next time your date asks you for dinner or for a fancy bottle of wine, don't assume she is using you. She may be disguising her sexual need with an advance reward, making this need look like a sexual favor.

Window of opportunity in bed

Some women are embarrassed about being the first to show their sexual desire. Fearing a compromise in her market value, a woman needs sufficient assurance from the man that he won't lose interest and stop halfway through the action. The purpose of foreplay is not just to stimulate the woman but to assure her that the man has a burning desire to finish the task in hand. A massage is one of the excuses some women use to have sex.

Many women like to start with five minutes of dressed massage leading to ten minutes of oil massage. Then shoulder and neck kisses come into play, followed by an earlobe lick, a few hot kisses, breast feeling, then breast feeding, a belly and thigh rub, soft fingering, and so on.

Then ten minutes of mutual oral sex and added foreplay lead to romantic love making.

I am not detailing this sequence to get the reader excited; I wanted to point out that some women are not comfortable showing their desire unless they lag a bit behind the man. A woman wants the man to take the lead and show his hand first, assuring her that his desire equals or exceeds hers. This sequence was most likely invented by women to camouflage their desire under the cover of unexpected stimulation and romantic love making.

An experienced man gives his woman the excuse she is seeking. She may claim to be drunk, excited, in love, returning a favor, or even succumbing to his pressure, and he will not disagree. If the man's desire leads too far ahead of her or lags too far behind, she might terminate the session. The window of opportunity requires the man to stay in the lead position but not too far ahead. Even a slight deviation might upset the balance required to accomplish the mission. If the man skips even one step, the woman might terminate the session or carry it forward with embarrassment. When that happens, the man will wonder what could have gone wrong. She won't volunteer the answer. She is not going to say, "Honey, when you touched my breast before kissing me, I felt very cheap because you exposed my sexual desire, uncovering the lust camouflaged in romantic kisses and sweet talk."

A young lady told her father that a woman can take the lead anywhere except in the bedroom, where it is the man's role to lead. He asked me if this was true in light of the commodity mind theory. I thought about it for a minute then I answered him affirmatively. The commodity-minded woman realizes that showing sharp interest in the bedroom could undermine her market value. Even showing a leading interest could also compromise her value. That is because sexual need, in her mind, is a debt incurred by the man, and she collects the credit. Showing sexual need could reduce her credit accordingly. If a woman is the first to show sexual interest, she lowers her market value in the man's eyes and could turn him off. Therefore she hides her excitement and trails a bit behind him.

Men and women differ when it comes to readiness for sex. While men are stimulated visually, women are stimulated by touch. To test this difference, consider how disgusted women can get when watching a porno movie. Since men are stimulated visually, their sexual desire grows when they watch suggestive dance moves by half-naked women in a nightclub. These same women need over a half-hour of physical stimulation before they reach the same stage of sexual readiness as the already stimulated men dancing with them. That is probably why "dirty dancing" became the rage in the nineties; partners could touch each other sexually on the dance floor to get the woman on the same page.

Sexual compatibility

An experienced man in his seventies had a girlfriend in her early forties. When I asked him about sexual compatibility, he said, "Young men are usually much faster than young women in initiating sexual intimacy and reaching climax. By the time he is done and turning his face the other way to fall asleep, she is barely ready to feel the excitement. As men get older, they slow down and become more compatible with middle-age women."

Sexual harassment

While on this topic, I would like to address the issue of sexual harassment. Men are stimulated visually while women are stimulated by touch, and sexual harassment law should account for these differences. Since a woman is stimulated by touch, touching her in the workplace could constitute sexual harassment.

Similarly, a woman exposing her body in revealing clothes at work place should also be considered as sexual harassment, since displaying her body has the same sexual impact on men as touching has on women.

34. Why does she resort to cosmetics, boob jobs, high heels, tooth alignment, and plastic surgery, or extreme makeover surgery?

Mother Nature made males of many species more colorful and attractive than females as a result of competing with each other to attract the females. As for human species, men have succeeded in reversing this role and convincing women to do this hard task and compete with each other for sexual attractiveness. What went wrong in the course of evolution that made this breakthrough takes place? It must have been the misappropriation of sexual attractiveness for goals other than reproduction that caused this to happen. Goals like power, survival, social acceptance, and financial gain contributed to this change. Wars could have been another factor that sharpened women's competitive skills to attract the few male survivors. Other species do not resort to artificial strategies for survival because they have not developed the commodity frame of mind. They wait until Mother Nature provides them with a natural change— perhaps colorful feathers, refined scent, or a better ability to build nests.

The peak of attractiveness for many women extends from ages nineteen through twenty-nine. With only ten years to set the foundation for a lifetime ahead, women face a lot of pressure as was mentioned earlier. Men have more room with a time frame extending from ages eighteen to sixty-five and beyond. They have about fifty years to lay a foundation. That is more than five times what women have.

The intense pressure on women to perform must have left scars on their psyches, and the commodity mind developed as a survival strategy.

Humans are the only species that has invented artificial methods to extend its shelf life beyond what Mother Nature allowed whether by the use of cosmetics or the use of Viagra.

35. What does she do to extend her shelf life?

Every experienced woman knows her relationship shelf life. It generally varies from three to five months depending on her skills and assets. How does she know that? She has seen enough relationships to know how long it takes a man to lose interest after the first sexual encounter. To control and prolong the relationship, she uses a set of maneuvers summarized below.

a. She seeks full control of the relationship and of the man.

b. She delays the start of sexual intimacy (I don't like to use the word *intercourse*; it sounds like a noncredit class) so that she can delay the start of the five-month countdown.

c. Every time she has sex, she makes it as difficult as she did the first time so she can reset the countdown timer back to zero.

d. She slows down the pace of the relationship so she can extend her shelf life.

e. She lets the man leave the table with an appetite so he will come back for more.

f. She spaces her encounters with him far apart to keep him hungry, but not too far lest he give up and look for other avenues. This strategy is intended to keep the momentum alive and extend her shelf life accordingly.

g. She hooks him on something else that is hers so he won't slip away. Joint assets, a business partnership, family ties, mutual friends, legal liabilities, and kids are just a few examples.

h. She lives with him if she can and gets him used to it.

36. Why does a woman treat different men differently? One can get her on the first night. Another can get her in a week. A third could spend a month or longer and end up in a contractual sponsorship for a lifetime and gets married to her.

Let's analyze it in the light of commodity market theory. Since her market value is her biggest worry, a woman spares no effort to protect and enhance it. First, she will evaluate whether the man is a long-term investment or short-term quick fix based on his assets. If he qualifies for long-term sponsorship, she will proceed slowly to hook him according to her routine agenda to get married. If he does not surrender to her marriage tactics, she will reduce her expectations and settle for serious dating. If he continues to resist her ambitious agenda, she will reduce her expectations further, settling for lesser and lesser ones until all ends meet for a one-night stand. One way or another, she will work the balance between her market goals and his best offer.

She will keep on negotiating a deal until she finds the break-even point between her highest possible market value and the best offer she can get. A playboy who presents himself as an enhancement to her market value can get away with a one-night-stand deal without making a long term commitment. If he makes her feel that having a one-night stand with him is a credit to her market value, she will do it and even brag about it. However, she will attempt to build on the one-night stand in hopes of turning it to a long-term relationship. She will surrender to a one-night stand if the man presents himself as a valuable now-or-never chance offering a potential increase in market value. Remember the rule in sales: the difference between rape and romance is presentation.

37. Why would a working wife keep all her savings for herself and not contribute to household expenses?

Some single women enter the working world primarily to support themselves while looking for a sponsor who will exchange sex for marriage. When she finds and catches Mr. Sponsor, her great-grandmothers' instincts kick in, leading her to quit her job and stay home while raising the children. Years later she might return to the working world to build equity for herself. That is clever. After negotiating a deal with her husband to exchange housekeeping and sex for sponsorship, she is now using the leverage of free time to get a second job at the expense of her prime responsibilities. She might think that she is working as well as fulfilling her duties at home. However, she is actually exposing herself to the stress and headaches of a second job, leaving no room for the spiritual fulfillment and moral support expected of her as a mother and a wife. Some men think that one way of achieving equality in marriage is by providing their wives with full financial support in exchange for domestic support. But a commodity-minded woman believes that exchanging sex for full support is the end of the deal and that any additional income she earns is her own. She thinks, *My money is my money, and your money is my money.* This is as far as she can reveal about this undeclared one-sided agreement known as "sex for sponsorship."

Relationships fail when expectations aren't met. When a commodity-minded woman is mistakenly or unwillingly sold below her market value, she will soon find out when approached by a higher bidder offering a better deal. She will then get frustrated and make her partner pay for it. She will have an affair to close the price gap or will exit the relationship and move to the new bidder. She can also make a man's life miserable through friction and irresponsible behavior.

Chapter 5:

Femininity, the Lost Power

God made man stronger but not necessarily intelligent. He gave women intuition and femininity. And, used properly, that combination easily jumbles the brains of any man I've ever met.

—*Farrah Fawcett*

Who is responsible?

Is it the fault of women that they are commodity minded? Not really. How could a commodity market exist without the consumer? After all, consumer needs determine which products do well and which products are removed from the shelves. We have wound up where we are today thanks to the coevolution of consumption-minded men and commodity-minded women. A frustrated man once told me that men are responsible for making women commodity-minded. Had men given greater attention to spiritual development and adopted more humane traits, more women would have been willing to develop the inner strength that could last a lifetime instead of settling for skills that barely carry them through the ten crucial years from ages nineteen to twenty-nine.

The basis of attraction

Unfortunately, many contemporary women have traded the inner strength of femininity for masculine power. Contrast is the basis of attraction between men and women. The more the contrast, the more they are attracted to each other. Men are taller than their women. Men are rude and women are polite. Men are aggressive and women are demure. Men have hair on their chests and faces, and women don't. Women have long nails and men don't. Men have rough voices and women don't. Women wear skirts and high heels, but men don't. Women have long hair and men don't, etc. As modern women try to match masculine power and therefore lose their God-given power of femininity, the attraction is lost.

To regain ground and restore the attraction, many women get boob jobs, face-lifts, veneer-coated teeth, and other external makeovers. But this does not work. The minute such a woman opens her mouth you realize you are listening to a man. As a result, more women are left lonely, without male companionship, drifting into relationships with each other.

As we continue to eliminate the differences between the sexes in the name of equality, women are becoming more masculine and men are becoming more feminine, leaving no room for attraction. Opposites attract. The more masculine the man is and the more feminine the woman is, the more the attraction. As Salma Hayek once said, "Sexy is not about not eating and patching wrinkles with wax."

Conclusion: Understanding Women; the Gate to Peace and Harmony

This book deliberately utilizes several case studies through commodity market theory to analyze inexplicable female behavior and identify the root cause of it. Inevitably there were numerous scenarios this book did not cover; however I encourage the reader when facing a puzzling situation to transpose any scenario into the commodity market model to identify a parallel root cause that lends itself to easy resolution.

Sociologists, psychologists and anthropologists might reexamine their findings in the light of commodity market theory. This new approach is merely the starting point as it lays the foundation for further research. Women are increasingly gaining independence and freedom throughout the world and are liberating themselves from the taboos of their cultures. This will increase their chances in taking western women as a role model by adopting their values over their own. With proper education and training those women can gain grounds but still maintain the roots of their own innate culture and tradition. Reviving the power of femininity is a goal social reformers should pursue to achieve equality not masculinity.

Dear young man,

With better understanding of your woman's behavior within the light of commodity market theory, you will be able to avoid communication traps and unnecessary conflict in most cases. You will not be checking out other women's bodies, while sitting with her in a coffee shop. You will not be rushing her out of morning shower, while she is fixing sleeping wrinkles, and applying her makeup. You will not expect to get laid for free, even with your wife. You will learn that the potency of your gifts has an expiration date and needs to be refilled. You will realize that relationships need periodical maintenance to remain vigil. You will learn that her sense of self-worth is dependent on the ownership and success of her children. You will accept that your role towards your kids ends at providing financial means and other liabilities. You will find that your actions and manners in public reflect on her value. You will know that ill humor and jokes that target her self-image is damaging. You will learn that she can not tell you about her sensitivities and needs because it will undermine her value. Love and affection as well as respect can not be solicited. You will then stand by her emotional vulnerabilities when she is feeling down. You will be more understanding and supportive when she is going through her middle age crisis. You will learn that her fluctuating mood is like a wave that you could ride on smoothly, instead of fighting against the tide. You will be more tuned to her feelings—not too far ahead or behind. You will realize how sacred her body is to her and will treat it with respect and appreciation. You will accept that sometimes she needs her space and privacy to do body maintenance. You will understand why her savings are her own and that your income is at her disposal for household and her expenses. You will learn to pay her sincere compliments about her dress, shoes, hair cut or beauty. You will learn that your growth and success at work is an expression of love and your failure will be punished. You will learn that unconditional love does not exist except in the lonely minds. And finally you will enjoy the ultimate measure of success; Peace of Mind.

FAQs Index

1) Why does a woman say that she wants a nice man who cares about her and treats her with respect but then get attached to a man who does the exact opposite, even abusing her?

2) Why do nice guys finish last or get ditched first?

3) Why would a woman give no attention to one guy while drooling over another?

4) Why does a commodity-minded woman want the man who genuinely does not want her?

5) Why does a woman chase you when you push her away and dump you when you chase her? Why does she chase you until you show interest and then leave you? Why do anxious guys get dumped?

6) Why do females use lame term of just wanting to be a friend instead of letting you know the real reason of not wanting to date you? Why not be honest to avoid him wanting more and not moving on?

7) Why do women like men who are self-confident, aggressive, funny, and popular?

8) Why is she never happy unless she is unhappy? Why is she always agitating problems and provoking arguments with or without a reason?

9) She brags about how difficult it was to hunt and capture her man. Why?

10) What constitutes a man's market value?

11) Have you ever entertained a woman out to nice places, showered her with flowers and expensive gifts, and had her turn you down for someone else who didn't treat her half as well?

12) Why do you get more attention from women when you are already in a relationship or when you are accompanied by an attractive woman?

13) Why is she friendlier with strangers while in the company of her man?

14) Why does she have a sixth sense?

15) Why do men and women have different opinions about fashion shows or strip bars of corresponding sex?

16) Why will a woman lead on several guys when she is not interested in any of them?

17) Why do women always go for men they cannot have, and reject single guys when they ask them out?

18) Why are nightclubs the most difficult places to pick up a date?

19) She doesn't know what she wants. She only knows what she doesn't want. Why?

20) Why does she say that she wants one thing when she really wants another?

21) Why would a woman say she is happily married when she is really searching for an attorney to get a divorce?

22) Why would she deliberately reveal her relationship with a married or committed man? But he does not do the same?

23) Why does a housewife attempt to possess her children?

24) Why does a woman insist on using exact change at the checkout counter, disregarding the long line behind her while searching for two pennies and a dime in her wallet? Most men do not do that.

25) Why do women always complain about men rushing them into a relationship while men do not have similar complaint?

26) Hell has no fury like a woman scorned. Why?

27) Why do commodity-minded women play hard to get?

28) When you give her leverage she uses it against you. Why?

29) Why does reverse psychology work well with women? Why does she like to do the opposite of what you want?

30) Why won't she give him what he wants until he shows signs of giving up?

31) Why would a woman choose the worst time to break up with you—when you are most vulnerable and most need her companionship and moral support?

32) How can you get laid for free?

33) Early in a relationship, why does she resist sexual advances and deny her sexual needs? Why does she hide her sexual involvement behind love, being drunk, being raped or feeling lonely, but never attributes them to sexual need?

34) Why does she resort to cosmetics, boob jobs, high heels, tooth alignment, and plastic surgery, or extreme makeover surgery?

35) What does she do to extend her shelf life?

36) Why does a woman treat different men differently? One can get her on the first night. Another can get her in a week. A third could spend a month or longer and end up

in a contractual sponsorship for a lifetime and gets married to her.

37) Why would a working wife keep all her savings for herself and not contribute to household expenses?

References

Barbara De Angelis, Ph.D, *The Real Rules: How to Find the Right Man for the Real You* (New York: Dell, February 10, 1997)

Ellen Fein, *All the Rules: Time-Tested Secrets for Capturing the heart of Mr. Right* (New York: Hachette Book Group USA, February 1996)

John Gray, Ph.D, *Men are from Mars, Women are from Venus: The Classic Guide to Understanding the Opposite Sex* (New York: HarperCollins Publishers, First Edition 1992)

Marcus P. Meleton, *Nice Guys Don't Get Laid* (Costa Mesa, California: Shark bait Press, Paperback Edition, June 1, 1993)

Mary Batten, *Sexual Strategies: How Females Choose Their Mates* (Indiana: iUniverse, May 15, 2008)

Robert Christopher, *Japanese Mind* (New York: Ballantine Books, April 12, 1984)